This workbook is to be used following the completion of reading

Jeremy Shares His Love From Above.

It will assist you with grieving, with your journey towards Enlightenment, and with living a joyous life!

The life you are meant to live!

Once you learn how to create your own happiness, no one can take it from you!

Jeremy Shares His Love From Above: Workbook

Copyright ©2018 by Rhonda Crockett Logue
All rights reserved.

No part of this publication may be reproduced, stored in a retrieval system, or transmitted in any form or by any means — electronic, mechanical, photocopy, recording, or any other — without the prior permission of the author.

The information contained herein has been obtained from sources believed to be reliable at the time of publication. The opinions expressed herein are subject to change without notice.

Edited and formatted by Carley Bennecke

Printed in the United States of America

TESTIMONIALS

"Jeremy's book and workbook helped me immensely in coping with the loss of my uncle. It has taught me how to not hold the pain in and how to progressively experience the natural emotions, knowing that he only left his Earth body behind. I don't know where I would be without Jeremy's messages and his books. Thank you!"

-Rosario Amezcua

"My mom passed away in April of 2017. It was one of the hardest things I have faced in life. I no longer had my mom, my best friend, the person I could talk to about anything. Jeremy's book and his workbook are helpful tools. I highly recommend them. They aided me with the processing of my grieving. It helped me to know that even though our loved ones are not here physically, they are always with us. They attempt to communicate with us, sending us signs that we normally don't realized or speculate about. The workbook is incredibly useful! I could not believe how much I wrote, including signs, questions, answers, and emotions. It's like having a healing session. I wrote many personal details that I didn't want to talk about or had a disbelief about. Grieving is a hard process. But after completing the workbook, I felt lighter and better about myself. It's a great feeling. We just have to remember that our loved ones are always with us!"

-Adriana Calderon

TABLE OF CONTENTS

How to Rise Above Grief When a Loved One Transitions	1
Let's Get Started	3
Step One: See the Signs	4
Step Two: Communicating with Heavenly Loved Ones	6
Step Three: Let Go!	9
Step Four: Let Go Again!	12
Step Five: Even More to Let Go!	14
Step Six: Connecting with Your Higher Self	16
Step Seven: Lessons Learned to Evolve	19
Step Eight: Dream Your Life *BIG*	21
Step Nine: A Beautiful Meditation	25
Step Ten: Be Grateful for Everything	27
In Review	29

HOW TO RISE ABOVE GRIEF
WHEN A LOVED ONE TRANSITIONS

Cry. Let it out. Express your hurt, your anger, your discontent, your sorrow.

Allow yourself the time needed to process all that is surrounding your circumstance.

Know that what you are going through is a major life event with many changes and considerable growth involved.

Ask for help. Don't go at it alone. Allow the support to surface, both on an Earth level and a Divine level. Accept the love you receive.

Discover the meaning of one's passing from this lifetime, the gift that's in it just for you. There is always a gift.

Be observant of those you attract, those that seek you out, and those that request your help.

Know that you will make it through this difficult time and will then follow the light!

Know that you will prosper and smile once again.

Know that your transitioned love one remains always by your side. They are safe. They are well. They are happy.

Know that you are Love, you are loved, and you always will be.

Take care of you! Rest, play, and eat. It's important!

Breathe, breathe, breathe! Breathe in loving support and exhale all thoughts not serving you nor moving you gracefully forward.

Love! Give your love. Express your love. Love learning the lessons you choose to learn in this lifetime just as your transitioned loved ones did.

Listen to us, your loved ones in Heaven, and follow our lead. We see you. We feel you. We know your path. We can help you!

Hear us in your dreams, songs played, and text read. We come to you in creative ways.

Be open to our assistance, as we can guide you gently on your path.

Know that we never left you and we never will.

When you sing, play, and dance, you will feel, see, and hear us the most.

Know all that occurs in our lifetime is divinely planned for us, by us and our loved ones, so that we grow, expand, and evolve.

Allow yourself to live the joyous life you came to Earth to live, experiencing all aspects of Earth life.

Move gracefully through Earth experiences. It's a choice to rise above grief or to be stuck in the past. Life is short, and you deserve to live the best life on Earth.

We are always with you, loving you, and cheering you on. Our love for you is eternal and is always blossoming, just like you.

We love you,

Jeremy

LET'S GET STARTED

When working through grief, one must understand the definition of grief:

> grief
> /grēf/
> *noun*
> The sadness, sorrow, anguish, pain, and despair associated with a loss.

In our case, we are dealing with the loss of a loved one's presence in their bodily form.

There are ten steps in this workbook; each step expanding upon the prior.

As you work through each step, you will begin to feel lighter, freer, happier, and more peaceful.

Allow the joy to grow! That is what your Heavenly loved one wishes for you.

Go through each step at your own pace, following your own Divine guidance and what feels right for you.

Always listen to you!

STEP ONE

See the Signs

Know that your Heavenly loved one merely transitioned (left their body), but they did not leave. They show us they are still here in many ways.

Remember in *Jeremy Shares His Love From Above* when Jeremy's cell phone kept turning on and playing beautiful music even after he transitioned? You may witness lights flickering, hear a familiar song on the radio, or spot butterflies. Our Heavenly loved ones are very creative. Unfortunately, we often deny what we experience. But it is your Heavenly loved one trying to connect with you to let you know that they are fine. The more you trust what you feel, see, hear, and know, the more these artistic indications will show up for you.

Write down the signs you have experienced (seen, felt, heard, smelled) since your loved one passed from this lifetime.

_____

_____

_____

_____

_____

_____

_____

_____

_____
_____
_____
_____
_____
_____
_____
_____
_____
_____
_____
_____
_____
_____

We hope that knowing your Heavenly love ones are still with you brings you some comfort and makes it a little easier to rise above the grief.

STEP TWO

Communicating with Heavenly Loved Ones

The main concept to understand when connecting to your Heavenly loved one is to *believe* that you can. Believe what you hear and see. Believe the information that happens to pop into your head. Rhonda initially wondered if what she heard was really from Jeremy or from herself, but she quickly realized that it was from Jeremy because it was something she would never say. *Believe*!

Rhonda likes to do *Automatic Writing,* which is writing down what pops into her head as fast as she can. You can do this, or you can just listen. At first, Automatic Writing was an easier way for Rhonda to hear Jeremy. Remember to do whatever works best for you.

Here's how you do it! Find a quiet spot. If you choose to be surrounded by nature, you will connect more easily. Our minds tend to chatter, but you can quiet your mind by telling yourself to only observe and not to share while information flows in from your Heavenly loved one. Take four deep, slow breaths in, counting to four; hold each breath in, counting to four; and then exhale slowly to the count of four. You are now ready to receive.

Begin to call your Heavenly loved one by name and ask questions or make a statement. Rhonda would often say to Jeremy, "I miss you," and she would hear Jeremy respond, "I'm right here, Mom." The first statement Rhonda would hear back, she'd write down. There should be no thought involved; the pen should seem to have a mind of its own, but it will be the energy of your loved one. Now, you try.

Call your Heavenly loved one by name. Write down a question and read it out loud. Record the responses that naturally flow through to you.

Your Question:

_____

_____

_____

Loved One's Response:

_____

_____

_____

Your Question:

_____

_____

_____

Loved One's Response:

_____

_____

_____

Your Question:

_____

_____

_____

Loved One's Response:

_____

_____

_____

If you do not hear anything the first try, don't give up. Try another time. Our Heavenly loved ones never give up and will always continue to assist us in our efforts. They know we will get the hang of this once we free ourselves of disbelief.

If you ask questions such as: "What are the winning lottery numbers?" or "Where did you hide the money?" then you will most likely not receive a response. Your Heavenly loved ones do not concern themselves with that kind of Earth stuff anymore.

STEP THREE

Let Go!

Holding onto grief will weigh you down. Your energy field becomes very heavy, making it difficult to move forward. With each step in this workbook, you will begin to release a little more grief, sadness, anger, and sorrow to free yourself just as your Heavenly loved one wants you to do.

You release trapped negative energy, like grief or sadness, by allowing yourself to feel what comes to the surface, what you feel in the moment. Once the emotions surface, you may feel tearful or angry. Feel the emotions and then thank the emotions that surface because these emotions were necessary for your growth and evolution. Then simply tell those emotions to leave by breathing them out. Healing can be as simple as this when we allow it to be.

Other emotions one might experience when grieving include confusion, rejection, failure, abandonment, heartache, insecurity, guilt, fear, overwhelm, shock, panic, terror, fear, anxiety, nervousness, betrayal, vulnerability, helplessness, hopelessness, discouragement, feeling forlorn, and feeling lost. Now it's time to release…

List ten emotions you feel about the passing of your loved one. Follow it with a time you felt it.

Ex. *I felt sorrow the moment I found out my loved one transitioned.*

Allow yourself to feel the emotions you list. Your loved one is holding your hand. Thank the emotions for their assistance in your evolution and for helping you learn your Earth lessons. Breathe out, requesting the emotions to leave.

1) _____

_____

2) _____

_____

3) _____

_____

4) _____

_____

5) _____

_____

6) _____

_____

7) _____

_____

8) _____

_____

9) _____

_____

10) _____

_____

The more you do this exercise, the lighter your energy field (which is you) will feel. Joy will begin to return, and your life will move forward in a better way. Remember that your Heavenly loved one is always with you. They never leave us. We can move forward with them.

STEP FOUR

Let Go Again!

Another heavy energy that weighs us down is regret. Regretting what we wished we had and hadn't done with our loved ones when they were here in their bodily form can weigh heavy on the heart. Remember what Jeremy shared in *Jeremy Shares His Love From Above*: our lives and our Heavenly loved ones' lives were Divinely planned, and we each played our roles perfectly to learn the life lessons we chose to learn in this lifetime.

I hope this awareness brings some comfort in understanding that every occurrence has happened how it was intended to occur.

Write five situations that you still have regret about. Release this heavy energy with enlightenment and love by allowing and requesting it to leave.

1) _____

_____

2) _____

_____

3) _____

_____

4) _____

_____

5) _____
   _____

This exercise is important to do every day until you feel at peace with yourself.

STEP FIVE

Let Go Even More!

Yep! To completely free yourself and move forward, you need to forgive yourself and let go of regret as we discussed in Step Five. You might also need to let go of the anger, hatred, and bitterness attached to not forgiving others in your life.

As you learned while reading *Jeremy Shares His Love From Above*, we forgive others to free ourselves and our energy, so that we have open space to receive the goodness that life has to offer. Remember, it's imperative to forgive yourself as well!

Below you will be making a list of people to forgive. Do not feel like you must contact the person you listed. This can simply just be done as a personal exercise. Make peace with your situation, knowing that there is a lesson to learn for your growth, even if the situation is terrible.

One way to forgive a person who is difficult to forgive is to hold a vision of a person you love very much (i.e. your child or spouse). Once you have a loving image in mind, switch the person to forgive into your picture instead of your loved one. This way, you are forgiving a difficult person coming from a state of love and compassion. Remember, we do not forgive for others. We forgive to free ourselves.

If you want to forgive someone in person, that is fine as well. But let this heavy energy go!

List five people to forgive and briefly describe the situation. Be sure to include yourself if you need to forgive yourself (most of us do). Then write, "I forgive (name of the person/self) to free myself," and let this heavy energy go.

1) _____

   _____

   _____

2) _____

   _____

   _____

3) _____

   _____

   _____

4) _____

   _____

   _____

5) _____

   _____

   _____

Repeat this exercise often to bring increased energy and joy. You deserve to live free!

STEP SIX

Connecting with Your Higher Self

Are you beginning to feel lighter?

Now it's time to connect with your inner being, your Higher Self, which is connected to your maker/God/Source energy. Doing this will return you to living your life of joy.

Slowly breathe in four deep breaths, counting to four with each inhale. Hold each breath in, counting to four. Slowly release each breath to the count of four. You are calm. Request for your mind to observe only, not to interrupt, and ask your Higher Self questions about anything and listen.

Some examples of questions are: "What will assist me to feel happier in life?" "What will assist me to move forward from the transitioning of my child?" "What will help me to move onto my divine path?" "Is my current job/relationship right for me?" "How can I live my best Earth life?"

Write down your questions. Complete the breathing exercise. Write the first answers that come into your head.

Your Question:

_____

_____

_____

Response:

_____

Your Question:

Response:

Your Question:

Response:

Make sure you are living your life for you, doing what you desire and not what others want you to do. If you are employed at an unfulfilling job, working to benefit another and not yourself, then you are not living for you. If you are holding back in a relationship and not being yourself, then you are not living for you. You are on Earth to live your Divine life, sharing your Divine gifts, talents, and Divine self. If you are not doing this, the time to start is *now*. You never know how much time you have in this lifetime, so don't waste another minute.

This exercise assists you in learning what is required to get back into the alignment with your Higher Self and your true Divine path.

STEP SEVEN

Lessons Learned to Evolve

Lessons to learn in this lifetime are Divinely planned. They are created before you enter the Earth realm as a baby. They are created by you, by Divine beings, and by others involved (Soul Contracts created) to benefit the growth of all.

With the passing of Rhonda's son, Jeremy, she learned the importance to love and live her life joyously for herself and not others. Rhonda grew by learning how to live on Jeremy's Heavenly level. The gift for her was returning to her Divine self and assisting others to do the same with the addition of working alongside her Heavenly son.

We receive Divine gifts from all Earthly events. These gifts are for your evolvement as Divine beings. There is always something to learn in all our encounters and in all our experiences.

Recall three situations that occurred in the past and write about the lessons you learned from each situation, how you grew, and the gift that was placed just for you.

1) _____

_____

_____

_____

_____

_____

2)

3)

STEP EIGHT

Dream Your Life *BIG*!

As you read in *Jeremy Shares His Love From Above*, you create your life by your perception, your emotions (how you *choose* to feel), and what you choose to do. You create your life, so dream *BIG*. The more you focus your attention on what you desire, the more your desires come to you. Unfortunately, the same is true for what we do not like. If we focus on what we dislike, then our dislikes increase.
Focus your attention on what you love.

List three areas in your life that you're unhappy with. Write about how you would truly love for that area of your life to be. Important areas in life to address might be in relationships, vocation, health and wellbeing, time freedom, and money freedom.

I would love (one area of your life) _____

to be (dream *BIG* and provide specific details) _____

_____

_____

_____

_____

_____

_____

_____

_____

_____

_____

_____

_____

Second area of your life to sprinkle the love: _____

_____

_____

_____

_____

_____

_____

_____

_____

_____

_____

_____

_____

_____

And third area of your life to change so that you love it: _____

_____

_____

_____

_____

_____

_____

_____

_____

_____

_____

Look at the dreams you listed every day and visualize yourself living your dreams! How do you feel? How do you act? You might feel happiness, love, and joy. Be observant and open to receive Divine messages, urges, knowing, and opportunities to act upon, which are assisting your dreams into reality. Give great attention and focus to your dreams and enjoy this process, knowing that your dream life is within your reach. You are a Divine child of the Universe and you deserve to live your dream life.

STEP NINE

A Beautiful Meditation

Remember that your Heavenly loved ones are always by your side guiding you. Rhonda likes to take short journeys with Jeremy when she is missing him. There will be hard days, but Rhonda has found that the difficult days occur less when she walks with Jeremy instead of without him. This short meditation helps Rhonda to shift a "heavy, missing-Jeremy energy" to a "light, fun, and comforting energy." Feeling and hearing our Heavenly loved ones makes going forward in life so much easier.

Rhonda lies down in a comfortable spot to meditate and she quiets her mind. Remember the breathing technique to quiet the mind. Then she requests for Jeremy to come and hold her hand. She feels the warmth of his energy. Jeremy has a navy-blue energy. He loved the color when he was in body. You may or may not be able to see your loved one's energy, and that is alright. You can ask your loved one what color their energy is and, the first color that pops into your head is generally the color. This color may change from meditation to meditation since energy is always shifting and changing.

Notice everything during this meditation. Rhonda requests and allows Jeremy to pull her energy up through the ethers. It's dark for Rhonda since her eyes are closed. She allows, and she doesn't resist. Your loved one will keep you safe. Rhonda and Jeremy then move past the dark sky. Rhonda describes it like opening a curtain and seeing a beautiful green meadow on the other side. Many times, Rhonda will see or hear other Heavenly relatives and friends. They talk, they laugh, and they enjoy the lovely flowers and their time together.

You can ask questions if you'd like. Rhonda is just fine being comforted in Jeremy's presence. Allow this to flow. The more you allow, the more of this experience you will receive. Jeremy safely returns Rhonda to her restful body, and Rhonda is comforted knowing that Jeremy is always with her.

Try this exercise if you'd like. Everybody's experience will be different because we are all unique persons. When you return to your Earthly body, wiggle your toes and fingers and move your arms and legs to ground you back to the physical world. You can do this exercise whenever you need to.

You do not have to live your life without your Heavenly loved one. Allow them in and walk forward together.

Lie down in a comfortable spot. Quiet your mind. Focus on the breathing exercise. Request your Heavenly loved one to join you. Feel them. Sense them. Notice everything.

STEP TEN

Be Grateful for Everything

Gratitude and love are the highest vibrations there are. These emotions feel delightful and heartwarming. This is because the vibrations of these two emotions are in alignment with your Divine self and with your Dreams. The high vibration frequency is the frequency that our Heavenly loved ones live on. To live a joyous life on Earth, one must live on that Heavenly level.

List ten parts of your life you are grateful for, even if the events were not so pleasant. All unpleasant events assisted you to evolve to where you need to be. Be grateful for all that occurred, as it was all Divinely planned for your growth and evolvement.

1) _____

2) _____

3) _____

4) _____

5) _____

6) _____

_____

7) _____

_____

8) _____

_____

9) _____

_____

10) _____

_____

Do this exercise every day for the rest of your Earthly life and notice how you begin to view only beauty and joy in all things. You will begin to glow, and others will wonder what you are doing to radiate this joy. Shine bright!

IN REVIEW

Your time on Earth will be gone in a blink of an eye. Our loved ones in Heaven are always with us. Choose to live your Earth journey with them. Follow their lead, consisting of the signs they share, the ideas that pop into your head out of nowhere, and more, as they see everything from their Heavenly view.

Let go of grief, anger, regret, resentment, and all energy not serving you. This energy is keeping your life stuck, making it difficult to move forward. Your Heavenly loved ones love you so much and they have only your best interest at heart.

Live your life well, enjoying and experiencing the many events you came to Earth to experience. Refuse to waste another minute in grief. That is not living, and you came here to live. Continue Earth life with your Heavenly loved one in hand.

There is no separation except the separation that you create in your mind. Let it go and live your life!

Live it *BIG* as Jeremy always says!

We hope you found this workbook helpful in rising above grief to moving forward on your life journey living joyously.

Angel Blessings,

Rhonda and Jeremy

P.S. Did you notice how many steps there are in this workbook? There are ten!

As you probably remember from reading *Jeremy Shares His Love From Above*, Jeremy says that the number 10 breaks down to $1 + 0 = 1$, and this is the *one* and only workbook you need to rise above grief to live a Heavenly life on Earth.

Live your best life!

Energy Healing is another helpful way to release the heavy emotions and energies associated with the transitioning of a loved one. To learn more, visit Rhonda at:

www.SprinklingSunshine.com

To continue moving forward with Enlightenment and Joy, follow Jeremy at:

www.JeremysChannelingBlog.com

www.ingramcontent.com/pod-product-compliance
Lightning Source LLC
Chambersburg PA
CBHW040044100526
44584CB00033BA/4273